FRIENDS
OF ACPL

P9-DZA-310

1/99

THE WAMPANOAGS

A TRUE BOOK

by
Alice K. Flanagan

Children's Press®
A Division of Grolier Publishing

New York London Hong Kong Sydney
Danbury, Connecticut

Reading Consultant
Linda Cornwell
Learning Resource Consultant
Indiana Department
of Education

A Wampanoag woman
prepares an animal skin.

Visit Children's Press on the Internet at:
http://publishing.grolier.com

Library of Congress Cataloging-in-Publication Data

Flanagan, Alice K.
   The Wampanoags / by Alice K. Flanagan.
      p.   cm. — (A true book)
   Includes index.
   Summary: Presents the cultural, social, and historical achievements of
the Wampanoags.
   ISBN 0-516-20629-X (lib.bdg.)   0-516-26388-9 (pbk.)
   1. Wampanoag Indians—Juvenile literature. [1. Wampanoag Indians.
2. Indians of North America—New England.] I. Title. II. Series.
E99.W2F53   1997
9744'004973—dc21   97-15090
                                               CIP
                                               AC

Contents

The Wampanoags lived on the shores of Massachusetts and Rhode Island.

Life on the Coast

For many centuries, Wampanoag (wam-puh-NO-ag) Americans and their ancestors have lived along the shores and on the islands of present-day Massachusetts and in the eastern part of what is now Rhode Island. Farming and fishing have been an important part of their lives. Always, they have kept

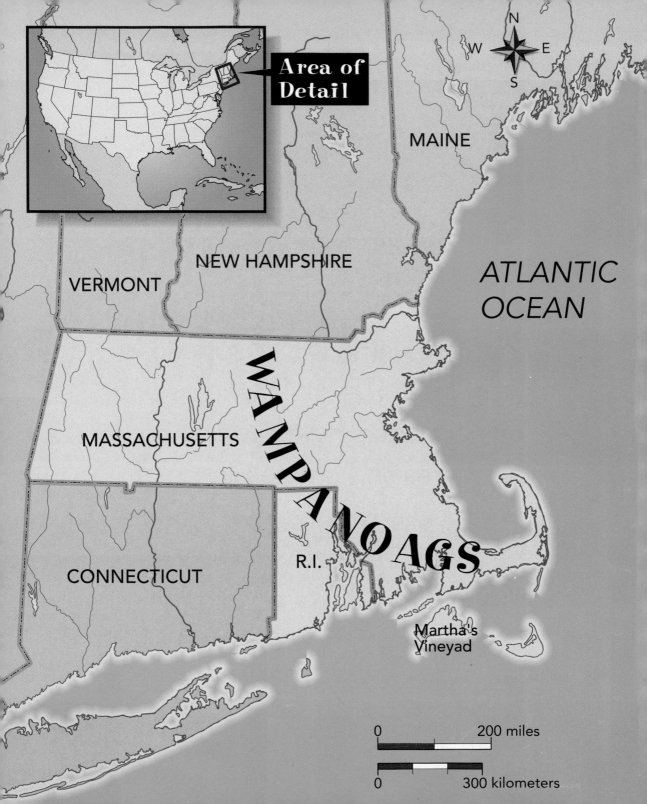

Area of
Detail

MAINE

NEW HAMPSHIRE

VERMONT

ATLANTIC
OCEAN

MASSACHUSETTS

WAMPANOAGS

R.I.

CONNECTICUT

Martha's
Vineyad

N
W   E
S

0   200 miles

0   300 kilometers

a special relationship with the ocean, the rivers, the forests, and the wetlands surrounding them.

Today, the Wampanoag territory is much smaller. The people live differently than their ancestors. However, many Wampanoags still live in or near their ancient homeland, and they continue to celebrate their native traditions.

One of their most important traditions is a play that

The cliffs at Gayhead are on Martha's Vineyard, an island off the coast of Massachusetts.

recreates the legend of their homeland. According to the legend, Maushop, a giant, created the colorful cliffs of Gay Head, Massachusetts. He was living there when the Wampanoags first settled in the area.

Maushop made friends with the Wampanoags and showed them how to live in peace and harmony. He protected them until the Europeans came. Then he disappeared. But he left smoke from his pipe (the coastal fog) as a reminder of the happy time when he lived among them.

Becoming a Nation

Today, many Wampanoags work and live in cities and towns. More than ten thousand years ago, their ancestors hunted with simple stone tools. Their game included the now-extinct mastodon, the caribou, musk ox, and giant beaver. They also caught fish

and collected roots, seeds, and fruit.

As large animals died out and people learned to farm, families stayed together for several months of the year. They no longer had to move so often to find food. As a result, villages grew larger and tribes were formed. Eventually, several tribes banded together and became known as the Wampanoag. They shared a common territory and way of life.

Today, the tribe is organized into five subtribes, each with its own chief. They are the Mashpee, Gay Head, Herring Pond, Assonet, and Nemasket. Their tribal councils work

Staff members at the Plimoth homesite tend a garden (above) and show how farmers dried pumpkin for winter (right).

together to protect the tribe's land and water rights and to improve the health, housing, and education of their people.

Hunting, Farming, and Fishing

During spring and summer, the Wampanoags lived in coastal farming villages. Only a few family members lived in small, temporary dwellings called *wetus* (WE-toos). Wetus were made of wooden poles covered with woven grass mats or bark.

The Wampanoags grew a large variety of fruits, grains, and vegetables.

In spring, everyone helped clear the fields so women could plant seeds. Corn was planted first, followed by beans and a variety of squash.

Usually, the three crops were planted together. Gourds, sunflowers, and tobacco were also grown.

After crops were harvested in the fall, hunting season began. People left their villages and moved inland to permanent winter lodges. The size of the wetu and the number of people sharing it increased. Sometimes, as many as fifty people lived together. Grandparents,

In the winter, the Wampanoags lived in large lodges.

parents, children, aunts, uncles, and friends all shared one house.

In fall and winter, hunters killed deer and bear. They trapped small animals such as

beaver, raccoon, rabbit, and muskrat. From the fur and skin, women made clothing. They dried the meat and stored it. Swans, geese, and ducks also provided food. Turkeys and quail were hunted, too.

From the ocean, rivers, and lakes, people caught fish year-round. In warm weather, the people fished from canoes. In winter, they fished on the ice. There were several ways of fishing—with spears, lines, nets, and weirs (wooden fences built across a river or stream). Along the coast, people gathered oysters, scallops, crabs, and clams. From rivers and

Wampanoags made dugouts, or canoes, called *mishoons*. From mishoons, they fished on lakes and rivers.

lakes, they caught shad, herring, and alewife. Today, some Wampanoags still make their living by fishing.

Sharing Food and Friendship

The Wampanoags are known for their friendliness and generosity. They open their homes to guests and freely share their food with others. This custom may have led to the Thanksgiving holiday we celebrate in the United States today. In the 1620s, the

Friendly
Wampanoags
welcomed the first
English settlers.

Wampanoags shared their
thanksgiving harvest with the
first English settlers in Massachusetts. They helped the
settlers live through the first
difficult years in a new land.

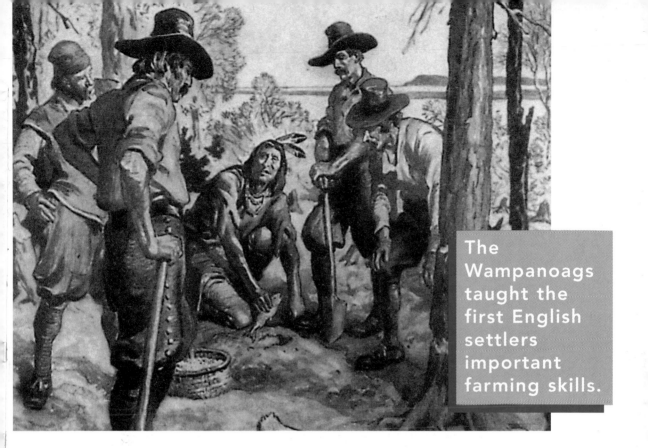

The Wampanoags taught the first English settlers important farming skills.

Because of the Wampanoags' help, the Plymouth colony in Massachusetts survived.

Today, the Wampanoag custom of sharing is still practiced. Some families even set extra plates at dinnertime, just in case a surprise guest comes calling.

The Wampanoags have always enjoyed many different traditional foods, which they prepare in several ways. Their main dish is a kind of soup made from corn and beans. To this mixture they add pieces of fish or meat and a variety of squash, roots, and nuts. They boil the soup well until it thickens. Stews are still prepared in much the same

Corn (below) was the most important ingredient in several Wampanoag dishes. A Wampanoag woman (left) demonstrates how a stew is prepared.

way. Today's popular fish boils and clambakes were a common practice in Indian communities of the Northeast a long time ago.

A Thankful Spirit

The Wampanoags have always lived in harmony with nature. They believe that spirits dwell in the forests and waters around them. Even today, many Wampanoags ask the spirits for help and thank them when they bring good things to their lives.

Many Wampanoags believe
that spirits dwell in the
land around them.

In the past, Wampanoags held special celebrations for events, such as a good harvest or hunting season, or the birth of a baby. In Wampanoag communities today, two annual gatherings are held each spring and fall or spring and summer.

In fall, some Wampanoags hold a Green Corn festival in thanksgiving for the harvest. Other Wampanoags have a Cranberry festival to thank the

Wampanoags celebrate the harvest of cranberries.

Creator for the first fruits of the cranberry harvest. In May, the Wampanoags hold a New Year's celebration to honor the earth's return to spring after the long winter.

Through prayer gatherings, called unity circles, the Wampanoags strengthen their ties to each other. Anyone can call a unity circle of family, neighbors, and friends. The singing, drumming, and feasting lasts from one to three days.

The Mashpee powwow, which is open to the public each July, is an exciting gathering. Tourists come to watch the singing drummers and

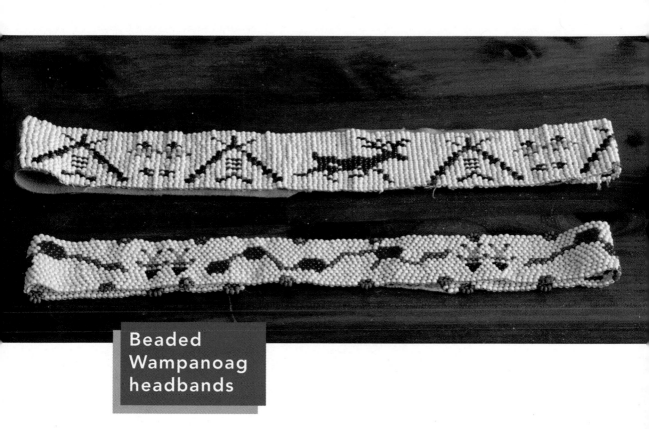

Beaded
Wampanoag
headbands

costumed dancers perform.
Afterward, they can sample
traditional seafoods and buy
native crafts.

Wampanoag

Wampanoag women have long used colorful clay from local riverbanks to make vases, cooking pots, and storage jars. Today's Wampanoag artists also practice this custom.

To the clay, women add finely crushed shells or stones to prevent pots from cracking when they are fired. They wet the clay and

Wampanoags used clay (far left) to make their pots.

Pottery

knead it like bread. Then they shape it by hand or on a potter's wheel. In the past, Wampanoag pottery was shaped like a cone. It was made that way so that it could be pushed down into the soft earth and stand securely on its own.

Today, most women bake their pottery in ovens called kilns. But some make their pottery the traditional way. They heat it in fire pits or bake it in the sun to preserve the bright colors.

Wampanoag pottery

Protecting a Homeland

For most of the 1600s, the Wampanoags lived peacefully with their English neighbors. Massasoit, leader of the Wampanoags, and other chiefs signed a treaty of friendship with the English in 1621. After Massasoit died, his two sons—Wamsutta (also called Alexander) and Metacomet (also called King

As a sign of peace, Massasoit and the English governor smoked a ceremonial pipe (left). During war, Wampanoags fought with clubs (right).

Philip)—tried to honor the promises their father had made. But disagreements over land ownership led to fighting. The Wampanoags could not stand by and watch the English take over their fishing and hunting grounds. They also did not want the English to build hous- es on land the Wampanoags had cleared for farming.

In 1675, King Philip led sev- eral tribes in battles against the English. He was killed the following year, and the fight- ing known as King Philip's War ended. By then, most of the Indian villages in Rhode Island and Massachusetts had been destroyed. The Wampanoags were scattered. The English

KING PHILIP

King Philip (left) vowed to drive out the English invaders. The photograph above shows Wampanoag schoolchildren in the late 1800s. They were required to wear American clothes and attend American schools.

sold many of the Indians into slavery and forced others to live on reservations.

Rebuilding a Nation

After many years, some Wampanoags began living and working in non-Indian communities. Some farmed. Most took any jobs they could get as laborers, servants, or sailors on whaling ships. In time, many Wampanoag communities disappeared. So too did many of their traditions.

In 1928, what was left of the Wampanoag nation reorganized, and its people came together to elect new leaders. Today, the highest ranking leader of the Wampanoag nation is still called the Grand Sachem. He is responsible for the people's welfare and appoints a supreme medicine man to handle all spiritual matters. Local governments, led by chiefs and tribal councils, handle the day-to-day operations of the tribe. They are aware of tribal events and have a strong voice in matters affecting the tribe.

A museum at Plimoth Plantation in Plymouth, Massachusetts, employs many Wampanoags to recreate Wampanoag life as it might have been in the 1600s. Here, visitors can see present-day Wampanoags dressed in traditional clothing demonstrating cooking, farming, canoe-building, weaving, basket-making, and pottery-making.

Men made dugouts during cold weather. They burned out the core of a log and hollowed it out with a scraping tool.

Wampanoag Americans

Today, Wampanoag Americans live much like other non-Indian Americans. Their homes, schools, and churches are no different than those in any American city or town. As concerned citizens, they participate in the government. However, to preserve their

native traditions and interests, they remain members of their tribal government and honor their ancient beliefs.

To Find Out More

Here are some additional resources to help you learn more about the Wampanoags:

 **Books**

Fradin, Dennis. **Massachusetts.** Children's Press, 1994.

Lyback, Johanna R. **Indian Legends.** Tipi Press, 1994.

Miller, Jay. **American Indian Festivals.** Children's Press, 1996.

Miller, Jay. **American Indian Families.** Children's Press, 1996.

Organizations and Online Sites

First Nations Histories
http://www.dickshovel. com/Compacts.html

This site provides short histories of more than twenty American Indian Tribes.

Mashpee Indian Site
http://www.capecod.net/ mashpeecoc/mashpe2.html

This is the homesite to a group of Wampanoags who originally lived on Cape Cod.

Mashpee Wampanoag Indian Artist
http://www.realbodies. com/rpeters/

A contemporary Wampanoag artist uses this site to illustrate Wampanoag approaches to pottery and art.

Native American Nations
http://info.pitt.edu/ ~lmitten/nations.html

A central site that lists American Indian tribes and links to their sites.

Native American Navigator
http://www.ilt.columbia. edu/k12/naha/nanav.html

A general site that gives hundreds of links to topics on Native Americans.

Native Americans
http://falcon.jmu.edu/ ~ramseyil/native.htm

A site that lists groups and addresses for those interested in Native Americans.

Plimoth Plantation
P.O. Box 1620
Plymouth, MA 02362
http://media3.com/ plymouth/plant.htm

This site provides information about a recreated pilgrim settlement in Massachusetts that includes a Wampanoag village staffed by Wampanoags.

Wampanoag History
http://dickshovel.netgate. net/wampa.html

This site offers a detailed history of the Wampanoag tribe.

Important Words

fire to harden clay pottery with extremely high levels of heat

Grand Sachem leader of the Wampanoags

Green Corn Festival celebration held at the end of the harvest

harvest to gather crops or fruits when they are fully grown

reservation area of land where American Indians were forced to live

unity circle a group of family and friends that is called together for prayer and ceremonies

weir a fence set in a river or stream to trap fish

wetu dwelling made from wooden poles covered with grass or bark

Index

Meet the Author

Alice Flanagan thinks of the world as an open book filled with living stories. As an author, she thinks of herself as an observer—one who watches the stories as they unfold, then carefully writes them down.

Once a teacher, Ms. Flanagan taught Native American children in South Dakota and New Mexico. She feels blessed by the wonderful gifts they shared. Now, through her writing, she tries to pass these gifts on to others. In the True Book: Native Americans series, Ms. Flanagan is the author of the following titles. *The Eskimo, The Chippewa, The Navajo, The Nez Perce, The Pueblos, The Shawnee, The Sioux, The Tlingit, The Utes, The Wampanoags,* and *The Zunis.* Ms. Flanagan lives with her husband in Chicago, Illinois.